THE ÆSTHETIC MOVEMENT & THE ARTS AND CRAFTS MOVEMENT.

EDITED BY PETER STANSKY AND RODNEY SHEWAN. FORTY-EIGHT OF THE MOST IMPORTANT BOOKS, REPRINTED IN THIRTY-EIGHT VOLUMES. GARLAND PUBLISHING, INC.

MODERN ORNAMENTATION

CHRISTOPHER DRESSER

GARLAND PUBLISHING, INC.
NEW YORK & LONDON
1978

Bibliographical note:

this facsimile has been made
from a copy in the
British Library
(Cup.1249.b.15)

Library of Congress Cataloging in Publication Data

Dresser, Christopher.
  Modern ornamentation.

  (The Aesthetic movement & the arts and crafts movement)
  1. Design, Decorative. 2. Arts and crafts movement.
I. Title. II. Series.
NK1530.D73   745.4   76-17771
ISBN 0-8240-2475-3

PRINTED IN THE UNITED STATES OF AMERICA

MODERN ORNAMENTATION.

MODERN ORNAMENTATION,

BEING

A Series of Original Designs

For the Patterns of Textile Fabrics, for the Ornamentation of Manufactures in Wood, Metal, Pottery, &c.; also for the Decoration of Walls & Ceilings and other Flat Surfaces.

BY

CHR DRESSER, PH. D., &c.

(AUTHOR OF "THE ART OF DECORATIVE DESIGN," "JAPAN: ITS ARCHITECTURE, ARTS," etc.)

B. T. BATSFORD, 52, HIGH HOLBORN, LONDON,
1886.

INTRODUCTION.

THIS Work has been prepared with the hope that it may be of service to Manufacturers who are engaged in the production of Figured Objects, and to Architects and Designers who have to produce the Patterns which Manufacturers require.

However creative our minds may be, we are all glad to have the thoughts of others brought before us for consideration; and by contemplating strange works, and, if I may so express myself, re-digesting them, we often originate things differing widely from what gave rise to the thought, and imbued with all the special characters of our own minds. In this way it is hoped the present Work may be found useful.

For some purposes the Patterns given in this Work might be used almost as they are. Thus the Designs on Plates 1 and 6 could readily be adapted as Wall Panels or Curtains; the central figure on Plate 2 would do for a Frieze; Plates 16 and 24 would furnish Dados; the ornaments on Plate 38, and the upper composition on Plate 5, would do for Ceiling Centres, either as relief ornaments or for flat decoration; while the upper figure on Plate 2 would serve as a simple decoration for the entire Ceiling of a Small Room. Plate 3 gives what would make a grotesque Border for the Dado of a Smoking Room; Plate 22 an ornament which might be similarly used where less grotesqueness is desired; and Plates 35 and 41, what could be used where grotesqueness must not intrude. The patterns on Plates 4, 13, and 14, could be applied as Damask Hangings; those on Plates 9 and 28, as Lace; those on Plates 19 and 34, as Carpets; those on 29 and 40, as Linoleums and Floor Cloths; the lower border, and that immediately above it at the left on Plate 5, for Carved Stone Work; and so on. These instances have been given only as a few suggestions for the use of our Ornaments.

The Author, as a designer of Decorations for Buildings, and of Patterns for Manufacturers, must of necessity employ a number of Assistants and Pupils in his Offices. The Patterns now published are all original designs which are the work of the Author, his Assistants, and his Pupils collectively. All are the result of the Author's suggestions, or have been produced under his observation, but some are from the pencil of those who have passed beyond the condition of the tyro. The Book represents but one phase, however, of our Office work, for in it are no examples of Architectural work, of designs for Furniture, Glass, Earthenware, Metal work, or the numerous other things that emanate from the studio, for it was thought desirable to almost confine it to Flat Ornament.

It has also been considered advisable to avoid those classes of Patterns which have been well represented during recent years in other works, as well as those which by much mingling of forms often produce charming effects when richly coloured, but can scarcely be said to consist of Ornamental Forms.

Decorative Designs are either original in their character, or are founded on some Historic Style of Ornament. The following gives the character of each composition.

The Styles of Ornament represented on each Plate are:

PLATE 1.—Persian.

  „   2.—The central figure with the two side-borderings are in the Gothic, or Mediæval Style, but the other figures are scarcely of definite character.

  „   3.—In no special historic style.

  „   4.—All the ornaments are in that style which the Persian potters took with them to the Island of Rhodes, in Greece. It may be called the Rhodian Style.

  „   5.—The semicircular ornament at the top of the plate is Egyptian, while the bottom border and that immediately above it, on the left, are Gothic in character: the other two are scarcely in any style, but that on the right (the broader), is somewhat Arabian in its features.

  „   6.—This is not in any pure style, but has many of the characters of Arabian ornament.

  „   7.—The two top circular ornaments are pure Persian in style: the two borders at the left side are Gothic; the little cross in the centre of the sheet, the little border at the bottom on the left side, and that in the angle at the right, are Celtic in character; the other border is not in any pure style, while the large circular ornament is a mere fancy composition, intended to give an expression of night.

       8.—This Plate is in the Gothic style.

PLATE 9.—These designs are in a style of ornament formerly used by the Venetians on lace.

„ 10.—None on this plate are in pure historic style, save that at the bottom left-hand corner, which is Indian.

„ 11.—This plate is of Greek character, the style being somewhat freely rendered.

„ 12.—The large circular figure is Japanese.

„ 13.—The three patterns on this page are formed of Cyngalese ornament.

„ 14.—Each design is Persian in style, but that in the lower left-hand corner is slightly impure in its character, having a taint of the Siamese feeling about it.

„ 15.—The two little patterns in the right and left-hand upper corners are Persian, while all the others are such as we find in the various periods of what we call Christian Art, the large central figure being in the style of the 13th Century.

„ 16.—This plate is purely Persian in style.

„ 17.—Pure Arabian.

„ 18.—The designs on this sheet are founded on specimens of old Venetian lace, but are not altogether pure in character. The small central figure at the bottom of the plate is Mediæval in feeling.

„ 19.—The three designs are Indian in style.

„ 20.—In no historic style, but was derived from the frost on a window-pane in winter.

„ 21.—The designs on this plate are in the Greek style, the right-hand upper figure being less pure in character than the other two.

„ 22.—This ornament is purely Celtic in style.

„ 23.—Ornaments in the Mediæval style.

„ 24.—Pure Persian.

„ 25.—In the style of the illuminations of certain Early English Manuscripts.

„ 26.—In no Historic style. The upper figure is intended to give the idea of evening; the lower is a mere drôlerie.

„ 27.—The two compositions on this plate are Mediæval in feeling.

„ 28.—These are from scraps of old lace.

„ 29.—Each design on this sheet is purely Mediæval in style.

„ 30.—The border and centre here given are in the Persian style.

„ 31.—Is in the purest old Persian style.

„ 32.—The right-hand top corner figure and the larger design below are pure Japanese: the other is composed of Moorish figures.

„ 33.—The three bands figured on this plate are Mediæval in their feeling.

„ 34.—These are not pure, but are in the spirit of certain Gothic ornaments.

„ 35.—That crossing the centre of the page is of pure Ancient Persian style: the small ornament in the upper line is Indian, while the other three are Arabian in character.

„ 36.—All but the bottom figure are in pure Persian: it is in no historic style.

„ 37.—All are Arabian in character, the two bottom borders being less pure.

„ 38.—In the Greek style, the upper figure being somewhat free in treatment.

„ 39.—The upper ornament is Indian, the lower is not pure in character.

„ 40.—The three designs are Mediæval.

„ 41.—All are in Mediæval styles; the central being pure 13th Century ornament.

PLATE 42.—These are in the style of some Italian inlaid wood-work of the 17th Century.

    ,,   43.—The upper figure is in the German Gothic style, and the lower is Venetian ornament.

    ,,   44.—A kind of German Gothic.

    ,,   45.—All four are in the Celtic, or very early English Christian style.

    ,,   46.—The upper design on this plate is in the Arabian style, and the lower in that of Turkestan.

    ,,   47.—This is a form of Italian Renaissance ornament.

    ,,   48.—Both are Roman in style.

    ,,   49.—The two designs on this page are Gothic in character.

    ,,   50.—Both are in Greek ornament somewhat freely rendered.

CHR DRESSER.

WELLESLEY STUDIO,
BRUNSWICK ROAD, SUTTON, SURREY.
October, 1886.

Plate 2.

C.F.Kell Photo-Litho London E.C.

Plate 3

C.f. Kell Photo-litho London. E.C.

Plate 4

C.F.Kell Photo-Litho London E.C.

Plate 5.

Plate 6.

C.F. Kell Photo-Litho London E.C.

Plate 7.

NIGHT

Plate 8

C.F. Kell Photo-Litho London E.C.

Plate 9.

Plate 10.

Plate 11.

C.F. Kell. Photo-Litho London. E.C.

C.F. Kell Photo-Litho London E.C.

C.F.Kell Photo-Litho London E.C.

Plate 15

Plate 17.

Plate 19.

Plate 20

Plate 21.

C.F.Kell Photo-Litho London E.C.

Plate 22.

MODERN ORNAMENTATION.

Plate 23

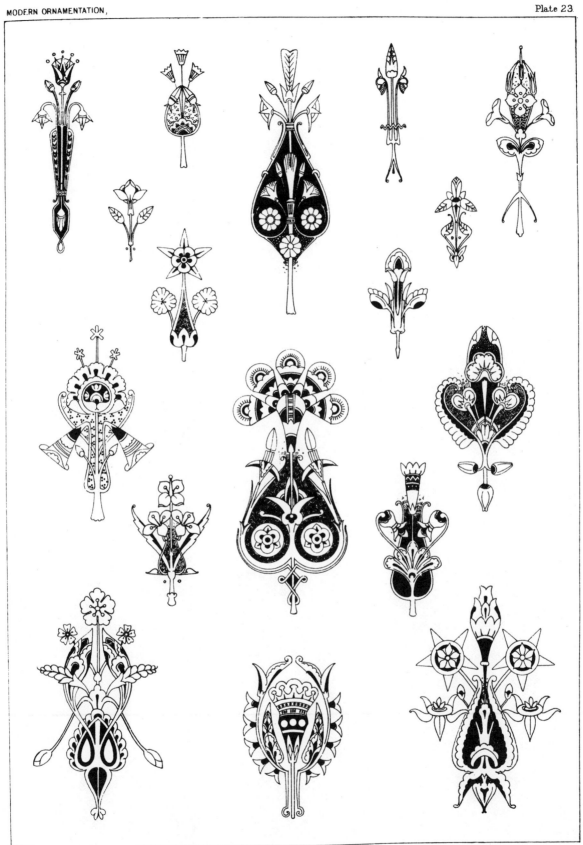

C.F. Kell Photo-Litho London E.C.

Plate 24.

Plate 25.

C.F.Kell Photo-Litho London E.C.

Plate 27.

C.F. Kell Photo-Litho London E.C.

C.F.Kell Photo-Litho London.E.C.

C.F. Kell. Photo-Litho London. E.C.

Plate 31

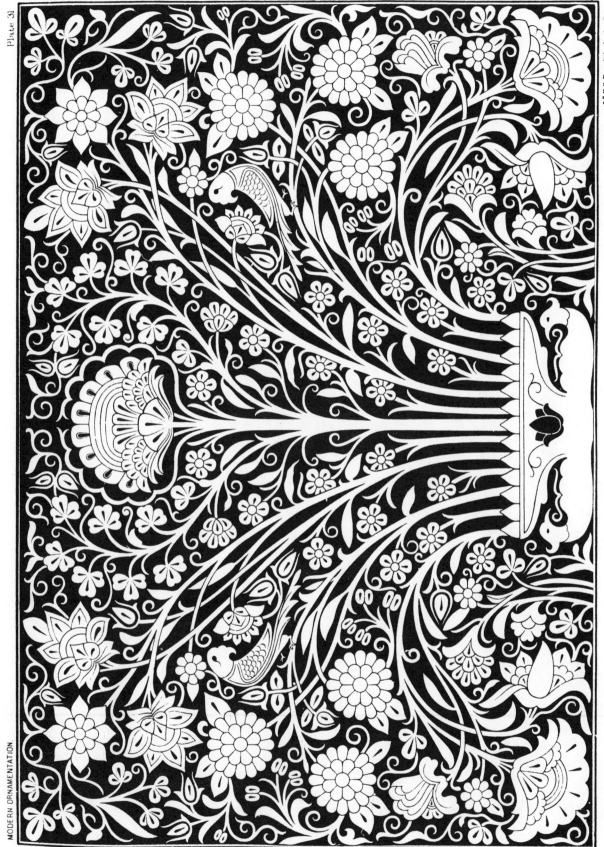

C.F.Kell Photo-litho London E.C.

Plate 33

Plate 35.

Plate 37.

C.F. Kell Photo-Litho London E.C.

Plate 38.

C.F.Kell, Photo-Litho London E.C.

C.F. Kell. Photo-Litho London E.C.

Plate 40

C.F. Kell. Photo-Litho London. E.C.

Plate 43

Plate 44.

C.F. Kell. Photo-Litho London E.C.

Plate 45.

Plate 46

Plate 47

Plate 48.

C.F.Kell,Photo-Litho.Castle St Holborn,London,E.C.

Plate 50.

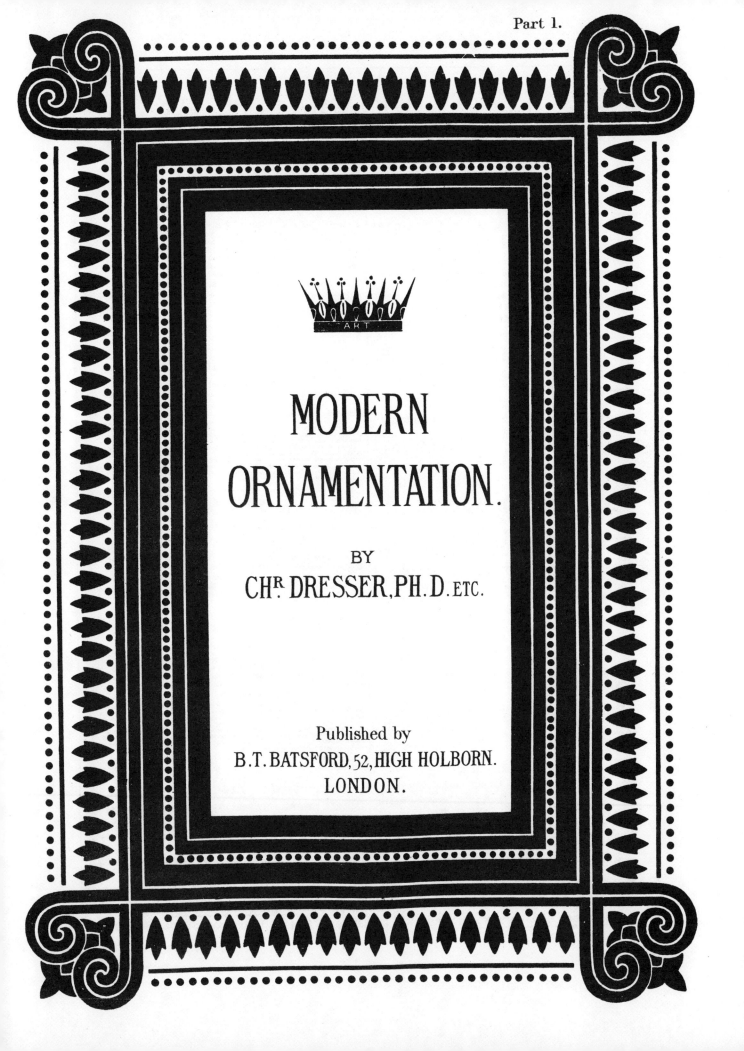

MODERN ORNAMENTATION.

BY

CHR. DRESSER, PH.D. ETC.

Published by
B.T. BATSFORD, 52, HIGH HOLBORN.
LONDON.